W9-AOY-081

## DATE DUE

| | | | |
|---|---|---|---|
| MAY 9 | | | |
| 3 Z | | | |
| DEC 1 0 | | | |
| | | | |
| | | | |
| | | | |
| | | | |
| | | | |
| | | | |
| | | | |
| | | | |

# How Do BIRDS Find Their Way?

by Roma Gans • illustrated by Paul Mirocha

HarperCollins*Publishers*

The artwork in this book was created using opaque watercolor and colored pencil on
Arches hot-press watercolor paper.

With special thanks to Charles Walcott at the Cornell Laboratory of Ornithology for his expert advice.

The *Let's-Read-and-Find-Out Science* book series was originated by Dr. Franklyn M. Branley, Astronomer
Emeritus and former Chairman of the American Museum–Hayden Planetarium, and was formerly co-edited
by him and Dr. Roma Gans, Professor Emeritus of Childhood Education, Teachers College, Columbia
University. Text and illustrations for each of the books in the series are checked for accuracy by an expert in
the relevant field. For a complete catalog of Let's-Read-and-Find-Out Science books, write to HarperCollins
Children's Books, 10 East 53rd Street, New York, NY 10022.

Library of Congress Cataloging-in-Publication Data
Gans, Roma, date.
  How do birds find their way? / by Roma Gans ; illustrated by Paul Mirocha.
    p.     cm. — (Let's-read-and-find-out science. Stage 2)
  Summary: Explores the mysteries of bird migration, including theories on how birds find their way and
how scientists learn about migration.
  ISBN 0-06-020224-6. — ISBN 0-06-020225-4 (lib. bdg.) — ISBN 0-06-445150-X (pbk.)
  1. Birds—Migration—Juvenile literature. [1. Birds—Migration.]. I. Mirocha, Paul, ill. II. Title.
III. Series.
QL698.9.G36   1996                                                                                         91-11918
598.2'525—dc20                                                                                              CIP
                                                                                                            AC

1  2  3  4  5  6  7  8  9  10
❖
First Edition

# How Do Birds Find Their Way?

Blackpoll Warbler

Northern
Oriole

We can watch birds fly from tree to tree, from tree to house, then back again. They seem to fly here, and there, and anywhere.

5

Snow Geese

If we watch birds all year, we find that some seem to disappear in fall, when the days get shorter and colder. They are flying south, where it is warmer.

7

Early in spring the first birds begin to come back. Every spring birds return north to make their nests, lay eggs, and hatch their babies. We say the birds are "migrating." They are moving from their winter homes in the south to their summer homes in the north.

Northern Orioles

Arctic Tern

Barn
Swallows

Once they reach their northern homes,
they will build their nests. They may build
nests in trees or shrubs, or on porch ledges.
Or, like the woodpeckers, they may bore
holes down into trees and make their cozy
nests inside. Some go to the same nesting
area or even the exact same nest that they
used the summer before.

Yellow-
Bellied
Sapsucker

9

Long ago people did not know that some birds migrate.
They thought the birds hid in holes in the ground and slept all
winter. Some people guessed that birds spent the winter in the
mud on the bottoms of ponds.

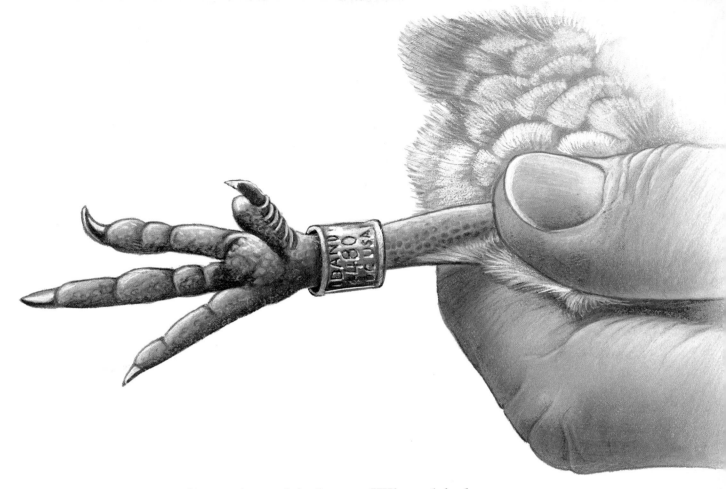

Now we know where these birds go. When birds start to migrate, ornithologists—scientists who study birds—use traps and nets to catch a few of them. They put bands on their legs and then let the birds go. The bands do not hurt the birds. Each band has a code on it that tells where and when the bird was banded.

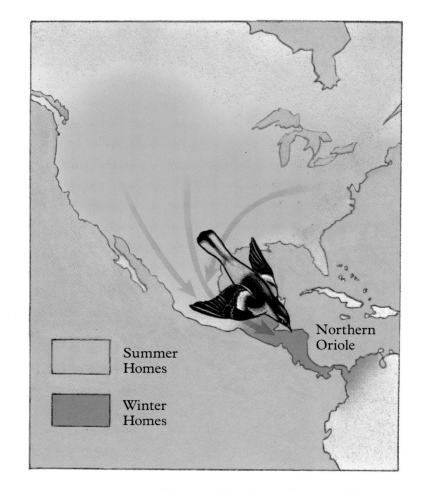

Some birds migrate for weeks because they stop along the way. Other birds fly for only a few days.

Some birds fly thousands of miles when they migrate. We know that orioles fly south to Panama. And barn swallows fly to Central and South America.

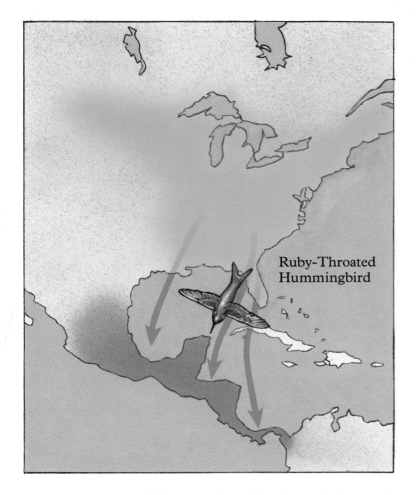

Ruby-Throated
Hummingbird

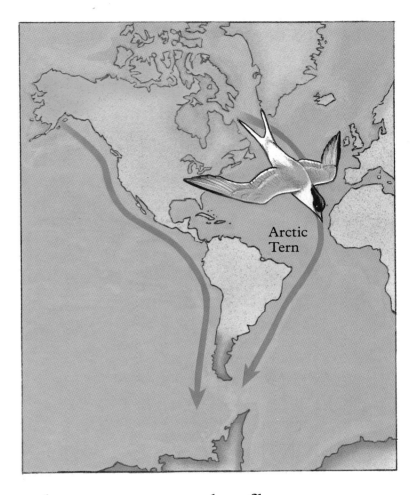

Arctic
Tern

Hummingbirds weigh only as much as a penny, yet they fly
over water for 500 miles, without stopping, when they migrate.
Arctic terns fly more than 10,000 miles—all the way from
Northern Maine to the South Pole.

But how do the birds know where to go? And how do they
find their way? That's the big mystery.

Barn Swallow

14

Arctic
Tern

Some birds may follow rivers, mountain ranges, or seashores.
But many birds find their way over the ocean. There seems to
be nothing there to guide them. What keeps the birds from
flying in circles?

15

Ornithologists have some ideas about how birds know which way is north or south. Birds migrate both in the daytime and at night.

Sunrise

When birds fly by day, they use the sun to guide them. Birds seem to know what time of day it is and can use the sun's position to find north and south. They know that to fly south in the morning when the sun is in the east, they must have the sun on the left.

Noon

Sunset

S

For birds to fly south in the afternoon, the sun must be on the right.

Blackpoll
Warbler

When birds fly at night, the stars help them to find their way.
Scientists have tested this idea. Birds were put in a big
planetarium where the position of the stars could be moved.
Scientists who worked in the planetarium placed the stars in

the sky as we see them. The birds flew in one direction.
When the pattern of the stars was changed, the birds flew in
a different direction. It was clear that the birds had noticed
that the position of the stars had changed.

Blackpoll
Warbler

But birds can also find their way when it is cloudy. They fly
when they cannot see the sun during the day or the stars at
night. How do they know which way to go?

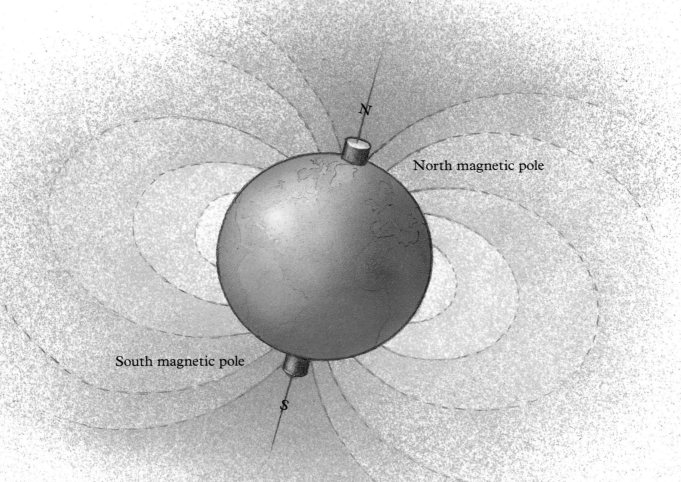

North magnetic pole

South magnetic pole

One idea is that birds are able to use the earth's magnetic field to guide them. The magnetic field is an invisible force that surrounds the earth. It is strongest near the North and South Poles. The magnetic field is what makes the needle on a compass point north. Ornithologists think that some birds may have built-in "compasses" in their bodies.

Homing
Pigeon

Homing pigeons are especially good at finding their way.
When they are taken far away from home, they are usually able
to find their way back. Scientists have experimented with these
pigeons. They put special covers over the birds' eyes so that
the pigeons cannot see clearly. Even when the pigeons cannot
see, they are often able to return home.

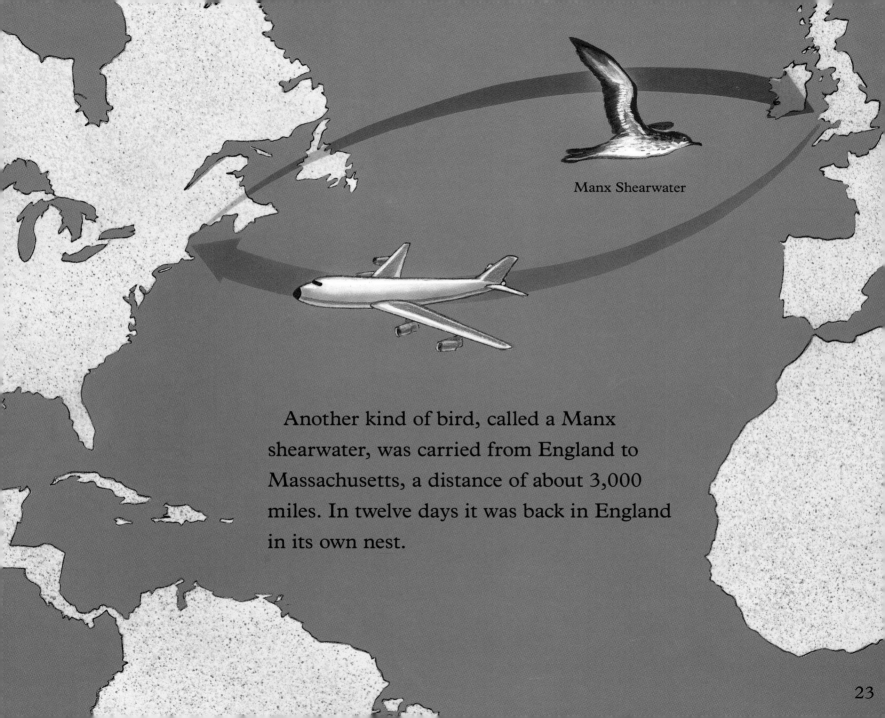

Manx Shearwater

Another kind of bird, called a Manx shearwater, was carried from England to Massachusetts, a distance of about 3,000 miles. In twelve days it was back in England in its own nest.

Northern
Orioles

How do birds know when it's time to leave for the south?
Or, at the end of winter, how do they know it is time to start
north?

Scientists know that birds have a built-in yearly "calendar."
This calendar tells the birds that when the days become
shorter, it is fall. It is time to migrate south. When the days
become longer, it is spring and time to migrate north.

Barn
Swallows

26

Yellow-Bellied
Sapsucker

Northern
Oriole

When fall approaches, birds eat a lot of food to store energy
for their flight.

All at once they are gone. They have started to migrate.

Ruby-
Throated
Hummingbird

Several months later, the birds are getting ready to migrate again. They must make their long journey to the north. It is time to build nests, lay eggs, and raise babies.

Northern
Oriole (female)

Northern
Oriole (male)

Barn Swallow

# HOW HIGH DO BIRDS FLY?

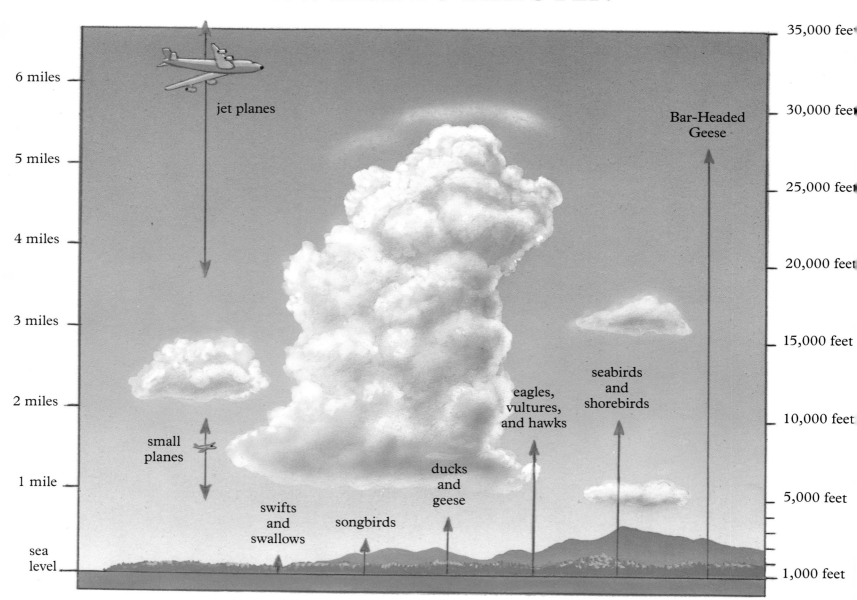

35,000 feet

30,000 feet

6 miles

jet planes

Bar-Headed
Geese

5 miles

25,000 feet

4 miles

20,000 feet

3 miles

15,000 feet

seabirds
and
shorebirds

2 miles

eagles,
vultures,
and hawks

10,000 feet

small
planes

ducks
and
geese

1 mile

5,000 feet

swifts
and
swallows

songbirds

sea
level

1,000 feet

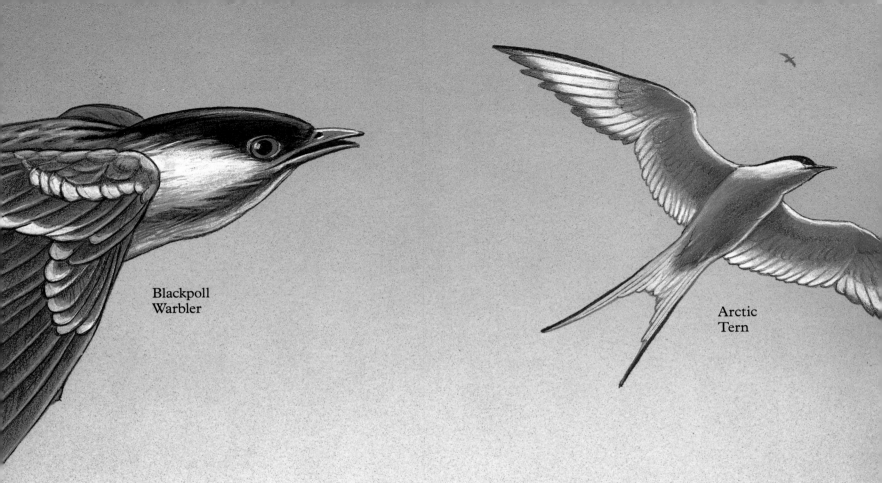

Blackpoll
Warbler

Arctic
Tern

We have solved some of the mysteries of bird migration. We
know where birds go. We also know how high and fast they fly.
Some birds fly as high as five miles above earth. But most
birds fly about a half mile above the ground. Some fly very
fast—over 50 miles an hour—when the wind is blowing in the
same direction that they are flying.

Even though people have watched birds for thousands of years, we still do not have all the answers about bird migration. But ornithologists keep trying—maybe you will be one of them.